Sisley

THE LIFE AND WORKS OF

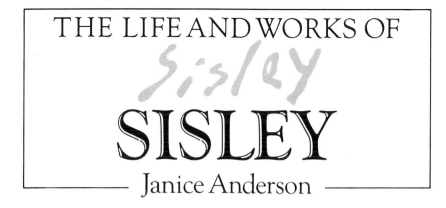

SISLEY

Janice Anderson

A Compilation of Works from the
BRIDGEMAN ART LIBRARY

Sisley

This edition first published in Great Britain in 1994
by Parragon Book Service Limited

© 1994 Parragon Book Service Limited

ISBN 1 85813 631 8

Printed in Italy

Editor: Alexa Stace
Designer: Robert Mathias

The publishers would like to thank Joanna Hartley
at the Bridgeman Art Library for her invaluable help

ALFRED SISLEY   1839 - 1899

Sisley

ALTHOUGH HE WAS BORN in Paris and lived all his life in the Ile de France, Alfred Sisley's English parents and his quiet, unassuming style, ensured that he would always be thought of as the 'English Impressionist'. He was born in 1839, the same year as Cézanne, which made him a little older than Monet and Renoir, a little younger than Manet and Degas. Although his mother came from a cultured, middle-class London family, his father's business background ensured that art was never considered as a career for his son.

At 18, Alfred Sisley was sent to London to follow an apprenticeship in business. But the teenager quickly discovered the work of the great English landscape artists, including Constable, Turner and Bonington, in London's museums and art galleries, where he also came to admire many European painters, especially the Dutch landscape artists.

By the time he returned to Paris in 1861, Sisley had put all thought of a business career behind him. He persuaded his parents to allow him to enter the studio of the Swiss artist and teacher, Charles Gleyre, where he intended to devote himself full-time to the study of art. Gleyre's fame had attracted many young artists and Sisley soon found himself part of a group of highly talented young men with distinctly revolutionary ideas about the purpose and practice of art. Some became friends for life, including Claude Monet, Pierre Auguste Renoir and Fréderic Bazille.

Sisley's earliest surviving paintings, dating from 1865, were quite heavily painted and tightly observed, in an academic kind of way. There were many still lifes among them, a form he was virtually to abandon in favour of landscape. For Sisley, landscape painting very quickly came to be the cornerstone of his art.

Much influenced in his early paintings by the work of Courbet, Dubigny and Corot – when he first exhibited at the Salon in 1867, he did so as a pupil of Corot – Sisley soon found himself much more interested in the ideas being pursued by the young artists he talked with in the cafés of Paris's artistic quarters: painting in the open air, reproducing the true light and shade in a subject, using colours as purely as possible.

In the 1860s, Sisley was able to pursue the life of an artist in an easy, untroubled way. In 1868 he married Marie Eugénie Lescouezec, with whom he had been living for some time, and Renoir painted a delightful study of the handsome young couple. But the Franco-Prussian War changed Sisley's life for ever. His father's business failed, he went bankrupt and died shortly afterwards. For the rest of his life, Sisley would be chronically short of money, never able to buy a house for his family and always having to move from one cheap rented house to another, sometimes not even able to afford canvases to paint on. He never seems to have considered giving up painting, however; on the contrary, it would always be his only source of income.

The inspiration for most of Sisley's art was the land of the Ile de France, the département surrounding Paris. He made three trips to England – to the Thames Valley, the Isle of Wight and south Wales – and one visit to Normandy. Apart from these places, a group of villages on the Seine near Versailles west of Paris and another group on the Loing south of Paris near Fontainebleau provided him with the inspiration for some of the finest landscapes produced by the Impressionists.

As a professional painter, Sisley considered himself part of the group who came to be known, after their first group exhibition in Paris in 1874, as 'Impressionists'. He was to take part in four of the great Impressionist exhibitions between 1874 and 1882, only deciding to go it alone in the 1880s, a period of particular hardship and difficulty for him.

During his life, Sisley never attracted the admiration or even the interest of critics in the way painters like Monet, Renoir and Degas did, perhaps because, compared with them, his style was restrained and quiet, his subject matter limited. It took other artists to see his worth, like Manet's brother, Eugène Manet, who said of Sisley's 27 pictures in the 1882 Impressionist Exhibition that they were 'the most complete and show great progress. He has a lake or canal bordered by trees which is an authentic masterpiece'. Of another painting exhibited by Sisley's dealer Paul Durand-Ruel later that year in Copenhagen, a critic noted that it was 'so delicately light and shimmery, so harmonious in composition, that one could find no fault in it. Here is no attempt to paint anything which could not be made out by the naked eye. The painting achieves its effect by means of airy lightness and unique beauty.'

Although Sisley had found some measure of acceptance as an important artist by the early 1890s, being elected to honorary membership of the Société Nationale des Beaux-Arts in 1890, he was never to know financial security through painting. As late as 1897, the year of his last trip to England and Wales, a major retrospective of his work at the Georges Petit gallery in Paris sold nothing. The following year, Sisley, himself too ill to paint, had to watch his beloved wife die of cancer. Less than four months later, in January 1899, Alfred Sisley died of cancer of the throat. He had called his old friend Claude Monet to his bedside, to say farewell and to recommend his children to Monet's care, and it was Monet who organized a gift of Sisley's work to the nation.

Three months after Sisley's death, the paintings left in his studio were auctioned to raise money for his two children. There was an unseemly scramble as dealers and art collectors fought to get his paintings. The re-assessment of Alfred Sisley as one of the great Impressionists had begun.

▷ **Women Going to the Wood** 1866

Oil on canvas

THE EARLIEST SURVIVING pictures by Alfred Sisley date from 1865, the year before this simple village scene was painted. Sisley was in his mid-20s and three years out of his artistic apprenticeship in Gleyre's studio. Since then he had been concentrating on painting landscapes, working in the open air, often in company with friends from Gleyre's studio, including Renoir, Monet and Bazille. Much of Sisley's time was spent in the forest of Fontainebleau and its villages, and it is not surprising that his work of this period should show some influence of the painters of the Barbizon School, especially Corot. (Indeed, Sisley would acknowledge his debt to Corot for some years to come.) As in this picture, Sisley's early palette was quite dark, his paint applied heavily and smoothly. Already, however, the Impressionists' interest in the effects of natural light on a scene is apparent.

▷ **Still Life with Heron** 1867

Oil on canvas

ANOTHER VERSION of this carefully composed still life of birds exists: it is part of the background of a portrait Pierre Auguste Renoir did of his friend, the artist Frédéric Bazille. Renoir showed Bazille in his Paris studio seated before his easel, on which is a large canvas depicting this same subject. At this time the three young artists – Bazille, Renoir and Sisley – were working closely together, each with his own easel and work space in Bazille's studio in the Rue de la Paix. Thus Sisley's still life, among the first of only nine he was to do in the whole course of his artistic life, is more than a simple, yet subtle, composition in shades of grey; it allows us a glimpse into the close companionship of these three young men, embarking together on the artistic life, ready to help each other, to learn from each other and, they hoped, to become successful together.

◁ **View of Montmartre from the Cité des Fleurs** 1869

Oil on canvas

THIS PAINTING of the view from the window of Sisley's apartment in the Cité des Fleurs in the new Paris *arrondissement* of Les Batignolles shows the artist continuing towards a style of his own. The influence of Corot and the Barbizon School may still be seen in the flat planes of colour and the rather dark palette. But what would become hallmarks of Sisley's style at its finest are more than hinted at here. There is the great expanse of sky over the painting, a quiet, greyish horizon and – most important – an attempt to give this outer Paris suburb a rural tranquillity. The Cité des Fleurs apartment was the first home of Sisley and Marie Lescouezec after their marriage, and the Batignolles was becoming a favoured locality for the young artists of Sisley's generation. Their favourite café, the Guerbois, was there and Montmartre, the main artists' quarter of Paris, was close by: the famous Moulin de la Galette stands out on the Montmartre horizon in this painting.

▷ **View of the Canal St Martin** 1870

Oil on canvas

WITH THIS URBAN landscape, a gently lyrical view of a canal in the heart of Paris, Sisley has fully embraced the Impressionist approach to painting. Gone are the carefully applied areas of flat paint which characterised his work of the late 1860s, such as *View of Montmartre from the Cité des Fleurs*. Instead, the artist has broken his colours into short strokes, giving a great sense of movement to the scene, and allowing a strong sense of natural light to pervade it. Even without the bare trees, we would know that this is a winter scene: the light from the sky, playing on the gentle ripples of the water of the canal, is soft and grey, thin and cool. Unlike his friends Monet and Renoir, Sisley did not paint many views of towns, for his preferred world was the country. But in this delicately sensitive painting, he matches them in his ability to evoke the atmosphere of the city. Others recognized the worth of this picture: it was one of two works by Sisley accepted for the Paris Salon of 1870.

◁ **Footbridge at Argenteuil**
1872

Oil on canvas

ARGENTEUIL, today an
industrialized suburb retaining
some market gardens, was, in
the mid-19th century, an
attractive village on the Seine
on the outskirts of Paris. The
building of a railway line in
the 1840s brought it within 15
minutes of the centre of Paris.
Its relaxed riverside charm, its
cafés and bathing places made
it popular with Parisians and
with the artists of Sisley's
group, attracted there by the
prospect of painting the effects
of light on the water of the
river and its tree-lined banks.
But the weather could not
always be sunny nor could the
water always sparkle, as Sisley
shows here. The waters of the
Seine are darker and more
grey than the sky above, the
men and women walking
across the bridge are well
wrapped up in drab-coloured
clothes, and the whole
atmosphere of the picture is
one of steady purpose, rather
than relaxed pleasure-seeking.

▽ **The Seine at Argenteuil** 1872

Oil on canvas

UNTIL THE FRANCO-PRUSSIAN War changed everything, Sisley's painting had been the greatest interest in his life; the collapse of his father's business in 1870 as a result of the war meant that his painting was now Sisley's only source of income, the one thing that stood between him, his wife and two children and dreadful poverty. For a time, the Sisley family lived at Louveciennes, away from the besieged Paris; the siege lifted, the young artists of Sisley's group returned to the city from the countryside or, like Monet, Pissaro and the dealer Durand-Ruel, from exile in England. In 1872, Sisley found a sympathetic dealer in Durand-Ruel, who began exhibiting in his Paris gallery such paintings as this view of the Seine at Argenteuil. It was one of many pictures of the village which attracted Sisley and his friends Monet and Renoir so much.

△ **The Small Square at Argenteuil** 1872

Oil on canvas

AT THE TIME he painted this picture, Sisley was living at nearby Louveciennes and often came to Argenteuil to work with Monet, who had rented a house with an attractive garden there and even kept a studio boat on the river, the better to paint the charming scene the river presented: it widened at this point, making it an ideal place for boating. But the village itself was also attractive, and was immortalized in numerous paintings by Impressionist artists. For this painting, Sisley gave himself a much warmer and sunnier palette than for *Footbridge at Argenteuil*, producing a charming study of the effect of sunlight and shadow on the buildings of this typically French village.

Sisley. 72

◁ A Rest Beside the Stream, Lisière de Bois 1872

Oil on canvas

IT IS GLORIOUS SUMMER and a young woman, possibly Sisley's wife Marie, sits under a tree, reading quietly. Sisley has dated this painting 1872, so it presumably was painted not long after *The Seine at Argenteuil*. Stylistically, however, it appears an earlier work, based on a rather darker palette and more heavily applied paint, from which the characteristically 'Impressionist' shorter brushstrokes are largely absent. Perhaps Sisley was compensating for the lack of the light-filled sky which dominated so many of his paintings: it is cool shade which is important here, given shape by the perspective of the vertical trees on the right of the painting and the stream on the left, leading the eye to the building in the distance.

The Seine at Bougival 1872

Oil on canvas

▷ *Overleaf pages 22-23*

BOUGIVAL WAS ANOTHER riverside village, a few miles from Paris on the left bank of the Seine, with strong artistic associations. Berlioz, Corot and Meissonier had lived there and Maupassant had used it as the setting for some of his stories. Bougival was virtually immortalized in a string of Impressionist paintings, especially by Sisley, Renoir, Monet and Pissarro. Monet's own painting *The Seine at Bougival* dates from 1869, when he began renting a house there. In this painting, Sisley confronts river, village and sky head on, dividing his canvas into three horizontal bands held together as a unity by the light which envelops them. As Sisley wrote to his friend, the critic Adolphe Tavernier, 'Objects must be rendered with their own texture, especially if they are enveloped in light, as they are in nature . . . The sky cannot be only a background . . . It contributes not only by giving depth to the planes, but also by providing movement, by its form, and by its arrangement in rapport with the composition of the painting.'

◁ **Springtime at Bougival** 1873

Oil on canvas

BACK IN 1867, Monet had painted a bleak, grey picture of Bougival in winter, with blocks of cracking ice on the river. Now, for Sisley's canvas, everything is transformed by the coming of spring. Two children, possibly Sisley's daughter Jeanne and son Pierre, walk across hills and fields in gentle sunlight. There is a softness about the whole landscape, with the delicately coloured blossoms on the trees echoed by the puffs of cloud in the pale sky.

△ **Louveciennes, above Marly** 1873

Oil on canvas

SISLEY AND HIS FAMILY lived for several years in Louveciennes, a village west of Paris in the forest of Marly, where they moved during the Franco-Prussian War. In the summer of 1871, from the vantage of a high point in Louveciennes, which was built on a ridge above the river, Sisley, Renoir and Pissarro had watched Paris burn during the Prussian siege of the city. Now, two years later, the view from Louveciennes down over the forest and riverside town of Marly is peaceful and serene. During his time in Louveciennes, Sisley painted many pictures of the village and the surrounding countryside, in summer and in winter.

◁ **Boats at Bougival Lock** 1873

Oil on canvas

FOR MOST OF SISLEY'S artist friends, Bougival was very much a place for gaiety and fun. Renoir, Monet and Pissaro had all painted the jolly scene at La Grenouillère, a bathing and entertainment place on one of the islands in the Seine near Bougival. Sisley, despite his love of country landscapes, seemed more drawn to the working life and industry of a place, than to scenes filled with people enjoying themselves. Here, he concentrates not on pleasure craft, but on a squat tug boat, busily puffing smoke into the cloudy sky, apparently waiting to go through the lock. It is another firmly constructed picture, based on two horizontals and a series of vertical lines; colours, as befits the subject, are darker and more muted than in Sisley's summer landscapes.

▷ **Louveciennes: View of the Sèvres Road** 1873

Oil on canvas

THE 'PERSPECTIVE' ROAD or path, narrowing into the distance or winding across the picture, assumed considerable importance in many of Sisley's paintings, because it enabled him to give a picture movement and a feeling of space. He has achieved both in this painting of a road in Louveciennes, despite the emptiness of the road and the lack of movement – even the two figures on the left appear to be standing still. Numerous critics have commented on this picture's similarity of theme with that of the famous painting by Hobbema, *Middleharnis Lane,* which had impressed Sisley greatly when he had seen it in the National Galley in London. It was a theme which others of the Impressionists also took up in numerous pictures. As with many other of Sisley's paintings, it is the sky which gives this picture great unity, its colours reflecting colours elsewhere in the picture.

◁ **Port-Marly, White Frost**
1874

Oil on canvas

THE IMPRESSIONIST painters'
belief in the importance of
painting *en plein air* did not
mean that they confined
themselves to painting in the
comparative comfort of
summer. Although Renoir is
on record as having called
snow 'nature's leprosy', most
of the Impressionists did some
winter-time pictures. Sisley did
more than most, because he
liked winter landscapes. For
him, the atmosphere and skies
of winter were just as attractive
and interesting subjects as
those of summer. In this
picture, he brilliantly captures
the atmosphere of a cold, clear
winter's day, so still that the
bare red branches of the trees
make mirror images of
themselves in the almost
motionless water of the river.
Where the sun's rays reach,
the light is clear, thin and
bright; where it fails to
penetrate, as on the snow-
dappled bank to the left of the
picture, the stillness is icy.

◁ **Fog, Voisins** 1874

Oil on canvas

'EXQUISITE' and 'atmospheric' are the sort of words that have been used to describe this wonderfully evocative picture. The bright colours of the bank of flowers tell us that this is a summertime picture, so we can assume that the delicate grey veiling over the scene is a light mist, not a dank, autumnal or winter fog. Perhaps it is an early morning mist which the summer sun will shortly brush aside. Sisley once wrote to a friend that he always began a picture with the sky. Even with this picture, he may well have done just that, for it is in the sky, with the patches of blue beginning to show near the top of the painting, that we can already discern the warm light that will disperse the fog. As well as this hint of the fog's dispersal, Sisley uses his painting technique to give the picture movement; his brushstrokes vary from place to place in the picture, sometimes short and brisk, sometimes longer and at an angle, but always combining to give vitality to the whole.

△ **Molesey Weir at Hampton Court** 1874

Oil on canvas

SISLEY'S FIRST VISIT to England as a professional artist came in the summer of 1874. In England, Sisley stayed first in London, near the Victoria and Albert Museum, and did one painting of Charing Cross Bridge before he moved to a small village on the Thames just upriver of Hampton Court. The village was Molesey, a quiet backwater popular with oarsmen and not unlike the villages on the Seine near Paris which had so attracted Sisley and his fellow artists. Among the 17 canvases Sisley completed at Molesey was this dramatic picture of Molesey Weir, the foaming waters of the Thames contrasting with the softer, yet vigorous movement of the clouds in the sky.

△ **Regatta at Molesey** 1874

Oil on canvas

SISLEY WAS TO PAINT some of his freshest and most light-hearted pictures in England in 1874; he clearly enjoyed the atmosphere of river life, for he set up his easel at Hampton Court regattas as well as this one at Molesey. Sisley has sent his brush, filled with wonderfully contrasting colours, across the canvas in short, vigorous strokes to achieve the marvellously active effect of the painting. Gone is the tranquil, leisurely atmosphere of *The Road to Hampton Court*. Now, virtually the same stretch of river is the scene of strenuous effort as competing teams of oarsmen bend over their oars. A stiff breeze, sending the flags straight out from the flagpoles and raising white flecks on the surface of the water, gives the scene a crisp note. This painting, now in the Musée d'Orsay in Paris, was for a time in the collection of the painter Gustave Caillebotte.

▽ **The Road to Hampton Court** 1874

Oil on canvas

ALTHOUGH HIS TITLE for this delightfully light and carefree picture emphasizes the road which runs along the river's edge from Molesey to Hampton Court, Sisley's eye was really on the Thames itself – the water road down to Hampton Court. This is a more tranquil scene than *Molesey Weir at Hampton Court.* River, trees and – above all – the sky provide a calm and serene backdrop for the white-flannelled oarsmen and the on-lookers, most of them apparently out for a pleasant summer's afternoon stroll.

◁ **Still Life of Wild Flowers**
c 1876

Oil on canvas

STILL LIFES DO NOT figure largely in Sisley's output, and those he did produce – birds, including *Still Life with Heron* (page 10) and a pheasant, several fish and some fruit – date in the main from his early years as a painter. This dark blue vase crammed with wild flowers has, in Sisley's hands, become part of a rare domestic interior, the subdued, subtle colours of the picture allowing the brilliant orange-red and pink of the flowers at its centre to stand out all the more vividly. The painting would seem to have been executed around the same period as two other still lifes – a plate of grapes and some nuts on a white table cloth and a basket of apples and grapes, also on a white cloth – which have been dated to 1876. Critics have noted how the blending of colour and the harmony of line displayed in these still lifes anticipate the work of Bonnard and Vuillard early in the 20th century.

▽ **Fourteenth of July at Marly** 1875

Oil on canvas

SHORTLY AFTER HIS RETURN from his extended visit to England in 1874, Sisley and his family moved from the hillside village of Louveciennes to Marly-le-Roi, a riverside village in the environs of Paris. Here, the financial difficulties which had dogged him for years persisted. In March 1875 Sisley arranged, with Renoir, Monet and others, a public auction of their work in Paris, in the hope of finding buyers from outside the usual group of exhibition-visiting art lovers. The auction at the Hotel Drouot provoked public demonstrations of disapproval at the work of the 'Impressionists'. Although 21 of Sisley's pictures were sold, the prices were too low – an average of 100 francs a picture – to do much to relieve his difficulties. Still, painting remained the only activity of importance in his life.

▷ **Place du Chenil at Marly, Snow** 1876

Oil on canvas

A DEEP, STILL SILENCE hangs over Marly-le-Roi's main square (renamed since Sisley's day 'Place du Général-de-Gaulle'); a heavy snow has fallen and now lies in a thick, white blanket over the town. Sisley's depiction of this scene is very realistic but marvellously subtle, too, especially in the painting of the snow, which looks white but actually consists of a fine blending of blues, greens, creams and greys. Pissaro once remarked that, in painting, 'the new is found not in the subject itself but in the way it is rendered'. Certainly, there is nothing particularly unusual or striking about the scene Sisley has chosen to paint. What is special is the way in which Sisley's 'realism' gives a mysterious and very special timelessness and universality to the scene.

◁ **Floods at Port-Marly** 1876

Oil on canvas

AMONG THE IMPRESSIONISTS, Sisley was the great painter of water. The floods on the Seine which resulted from heavy spring rain in 1876 provided him with the subject for his most memorable series of pictures. Sisley had painted this very point of the river at Port-Marly during another flood in 1872. Now, he comes back to the scene with great assurance, not simply recording a calamitous event in the history of the town, but producing a technically superb picture, in which he melds three quite different planes – sky, water and building – into a fine unity, using the clumps of trees and group of boats to link the square flatness of the building into the composition as a whole. Critics have had good reason to call this picture, which Sisley is thought to have included in the third Impressionist Exhibition of 1876, a quiet masterpiece of Impressionism.

△ **Floods at Port-Marly** 1876

Oil on canvas

THE FLOOD WATER has receded, part of the river bank and roadway has come back into view, some of the trees have got their feet out of the water, and the citizens of Port-Marly now have the chance to come out and inspect the damage. This picture may be Sisley as recorder of events, but it is also Sisley using his extremely sensitive artist's eye to create a picture with a wonderful harmony of delicate colour. He has used many shades of grey, counter-pointed with pinks, blues and greens to make a gentle study of the effect of the flood; he has even managed to inject a note of optimism, by adding the merest hint of pink to the tips of the tree branches, suggesting the buds waiting to burst out as spring approaches.

▷ Village by the Seine (Villeneuve-La-Garenne) 1876

Oil on canvas

SISLEY IS ONCE AGAIN confronting his favourite subject, the Seine. It is now high summer, the flood waters of spring have long receded, and the water level is well below the top of the river bank. The artist has chosen a favourite viewpoint, too, confronting his subject head-on, which allows him to divide his picture into horizontal bands: river bank, river, the far river bank topped with houses, and the sky. Another major Impressionist theme, the effects of light and shade on a picture, is also very much in evidence. Sisley's easel has been set up in the shade of trees, but much of the river and the opposite bank and houses are in bright sunlight. Trees at either edge of the picture offer vertical lines to break up the horizontal ones, but also contain the scene, to concentrate our thoughts on what is in front of us.

◁ **The Seine at Suresnes** 1877

Oil on canvas

THE SWIRLING CLOUDS dominating this landscape – 'skyscape' might be a better word – are so heavy as to make one think of some of van Gogh's landscapes from the south of France. Unusually for him, Sisley is attempting here to catch on canvas a fast-changing scene – an approaching storm. Although there is still the odd touch of sunlight in the scene, the river is already leaden and dull from the lack of light; even the trees seem heavy and lifeless. All the movement is in the sky. The picture is perhaps less successful than much of Sisley's work simply because it is not a quiet, gentle scene, giving the artist time to concentrate on depicting light and shade. Fellow artist Gustave Caillebotte must have appreciated its worth, however, for it was in the collection of paintings that he left to the French nation.

▷ **Tug Boat on the Loing at Saint-Mammès** 1877

Oil on canvas

THE YEAR SISLEY painted this lively picture of a boat at work on the River Loing, a large river which joined the Seine south of Fontainebleau, was a difficult one for him. He had sent 17 pictures to the third Impressionist Exhibition, held in Paris in April, and had failed to sell a single one. There were one or two admiring reviews, such as Georges Rivière's in *L'Impressioniste,* which noted that all Sisley's pictures 'showed the same taste, subtlety and feeling of repose', but on the whole the critics ignored him. No notices meant, of course, no sales, at a time when Sisley's finances were critical, eventually entailing yet another move later in 1877 from Marly-le-Roi to Sèvres. The move must have taken place about the time this beautifully autumnal painting, with its glowing mix of golds, greens and reds, was painted on the Loing.

△ **A Road in Seine et Marne** 1878

Oil on canvas

SEINE ET MARNE, on the eastern edge of the Ile de France, was to be Sisley's countryside for the last 20 years of his life. He moved to Veneux-Nadon, near Moret-sur-Loing, in 1880, having been evicted from his house in Sèvres for not paying his rent. It is clear from the subjects of his paintings, however, that he had been coming to the area to work for some years before he moved his family there permanently. It was an agriculturally rich and peaceful countryside, well wooded, and with many historic towns and villages. It was, in fact, an ideal region for Sisley to work in, far enough away from the turmoil of the artistic world of Paris to enable him to turn his back on such disappointments as rejection by the Salon (which had happened earlier in 1878) and concentrate on what mattered most: producing serene and lovely pictures such as this autumn scene.

▷ **Winter Morning** 1878

Oil on canvas

THE LINES OF POPLARS suggest that the river in this picture could be the Loing, rather than the Seine west of Paris, where Sisley was still living. Not that the name of the river is all that important; what matters is how Sisley has used it to give perspective to his cool winter scene, dominated by a group of trees totally bare of leaves. It is, for Sisley, quite a bleak picture, perhaps mirroring the bleakness of his circumstances. Just a few months before he painted *Winter Morning,* Sisley, desperate for money, had written to Théodore Duret, one of the Impressionists' greatest supporters, suggesting a deal. 'Might you be able to find some intelligent man . . . who has enough faith in your artistic knowledge to be persuaded to spend a bit of money on a painting by an artist who is on the very verge of recognition?' he wrote. Duret did not find such a man, but he was able to sell several of Sisley's paintings, thus relieving his financial distress for a time.

◁ **Snow at Louveciennes** 1878

Oil on canvas

THIS IS PROBABLY one of Sisley's best-known paintings, if only because its masterly evocation of a winter scene has made it a popular subject for Christmas cards. Once again, as in *Place du Chenil, Marly, Snow,* Sisley conveys a strong sense of the reality of snowy weather. He uses the solitary figure of the woman walking between the walls of a street in Louveciennes to convey that particular quiet which hangs over a place blanketed by snow. He has tended to be more economical in his use of colours here: there is a lot of white in the snow, though it is everywhere broken up by touches and light strokes of blue, grey and creamy browns.

△ **Path Leading to Ville d'Avray** 1879

Oil on canvas

SISLEY HAS RETURNED to an early haunt of the Impressionists for this painting. Ville d'Avray, near the great park of Saint Cloud in well-wooded countryside close to Paris, had been a favourite spot of Corot's: he painted several celebrated pictures of nearby stretches of water while living there. Monet had also lived there for a time before the Franco-Prussian War. In fact, it was Monet who provided the Impressionist story with one of its more telling incidents when he decided to paint a picture entirely in the open air at Ville d'Avray. It was a very large picture and he dug a trench for its lower section so that he could easily reach the top of his canvas. Sisley appears to have done this painting in the open air, too, but he leaves us to imagine Ville d'Avray by giving us a winding path towards the village for our mind's eye to travel along.

▷ The Footbridge Over the Railway at Sèvres c 1879

Oil on canvas

THE IMPRESSIONISTS were great supporters of the railway. They liked the way it brought them quickly into Paris, the hub of their world, and took them quickly out of the city again, back to the riverside and countryside villages that were the inspiration of so much of their best work. Among the Impressionists who used the railway as a subject, Monet was outstanding. He exhibited eight of his splendid series of the Gare Saint-Lazare in Paris at the 1877 Impressionist Exhibition, where they were no doubt seen by Sisley. Sisley's own railway picture, painted two years later, is quite different in approach. He shows a countrified scene, typical of the understated way in which he worked. Apart from the beautifully judged colours, with delicate strokes of pink lightening the low-key greens and blues, this is not one of Sisley's most satisfying pictures. It is realistic, but not realistic enough; the train appears to have no rails to run on, and what is that patch of pink on the embankment? A brief fire sparked by the engine?

◁ **Snow at Veneux-Nadon**
1880

Oil on canvas

HERE SISLEY RECORDS his first winter on the Loing, having moved to Veneux-Nadon – 'ten minutes from the station at Moret' he was to tell Monet a few months later – earlier in 1880. Once again, he is depicting a snow-covered world, dominated by a cloud-laden sky streaked with the rays of the rising sun. It was a scene he painted several times, rising early to record workers heading for the mills which were among the small village's main sources of employment. Once again, his painting has a strong sense of atmosphere, conveying well the early morning cold and quiet. He has kept his colours muted, the better to emphasise the distant, pale presence of the sun.

▷ **Veneux, August Afternoon**
1881

Oil on canvas

1881 WAS ANOTHER difficult
year for Sisley, financially. He
managed to scrape together
enough money to pay for a
trip to the Isle of Wight in
June, which should have
produced some fine paintings,
but his canvases never arrived
from France and, in sad
contrast to his 1874 trip to the
Thames area, he could not
afford to buy English canvases.
A hint of what might have
come out of his Isle of Wight
trip is given in this gloriously
summery picture, painted on
his return to France in August.
It is a familiar Sisley theme: a
tranquil riverside setting, with
beautifully observed trees and
a splendid sky, but how
cleverly he has handled the
composition. He has so
arranged the light-coloured
areas of the canvas that they
draw the two halves of the
painting together, for the eye
is drawn from the creamy
clouds circling the sky on the
left-hand side of the picture
over to the patch of sunlight
falling on the pathway on the
right.

△ **The Garden of M. Hoschedé** 1881

Oil on canvas

IF THE 'M. HOSCHEDÉ' of the painting was, as he is presumed to be, Ernest Hoschedé, a department store director who was an enthusiastic collector of the works of the Impressionists, then this painting could well have been done in or near Monet's garden at Giverny. Hoschedé and his wife, Alice, were close friends of the Monet family and after Hoschedé went bankrupt (forcing him to sell most of his Impressionist collection, including 13 Sisleys), they and their six children moved into Monet's house at Giverny. Ernest Hoschedé returned to Paris about the time Sisley painted this picture, leaving Alice to live with Monet. The two were married after Hoschedé's death in 1891.

▷ **A Path in the Gardens of By** 1881

Oil on canvas.

INSPIRED BY THE NEW scenery and places around him, Sisley worked tirelessly during the spring and summer of 1881 at Veneux-Nadon, painting meadows and orchards, village scenes, and, of course, the river. At By, on the riverbank near Veneux-Nadon, there was an old ferry crossing, with a disused towpath running alongside it; this became the subject of several paintings, including this delightfully light and breezy summer scene, based on a palette of blues, greens and pinks, lit by typically Sisley touches of yellow-cream, used to great effect on the right of the picture, where they give movement to the trees and draw the eye to the building on the edge of the water. Many of the paintings Sisley did at Veneux-Nadon in 1881 were shown at a major exhibition of the work of the Impressionists organized by Gustave Caillebotte in Paris in March 1882.

△ **Saint-Mammès** 1885

Oil on canvas

SAINT-MAMMES, on the Loing at the point where it flows into the Seine, was another resting place for the Sisley family on their frequent journeyings from one low-rent house to another. They had moved there from Moret-sur-Loing, whence they had moved from Veneux-Nadon, in 1883, and would stay there before returning to Moret, Sisley's final home, in 1889. Not that any of these moves involved great distances, as they were all within a few kilometres of each other on the Loing. The river was busy with barge and boat traffic here, and at Saint-Mammès was all the more interesting because of the presence of a dam and several boatyards. The latter inspired in Sisley the concept of series painting which was to occupy much of the last years of his life. He painted several pictures of the dam which appears in this picture and a number of the boatyards, at different times of day and in different weather conditions.

▷ **Barge at Saint-Mammès**
c 1885

Oil on canvas

THE DECADE OF the 1880s, during most of which Sisley lived at Saint-Mammès, was the most difficult of all his life as an artist. He sold few pictures, and his main dealer, Durand-Ruel, was himself in great financial difficulty and could not afford to pay the artist a retainer. Sisley had also decided that it was no longer appropriate for him to exhibit his work along with that of the other Impressionists, a decision which left him feeling isolated from his former associates and very much alone in the world of art. None of this stopped him painting, however, and the final tally of paintings he did in and around Saint-Mammès reached some 60 works. There is in the Louvre a notebook which Sisley kept at this time, in which he sketched the paintings he did between 1883 and 1885, often noting their size and to whom he sold them (if he did); this view of the river at Saint-Mammès appears several times.

◁ **Sailing Boats** c 1885

Oil on canvas

THE BOATYARDS at Saint-Mammès inspired Sisley to do some very lively pictures, including this colourful scene, which – despite its title – appears to show several river pleasure craft, tied up next to a barge with lifting gear. The picture is a favourite Sisley composition, in which the subject is confronted head-on and the picture is divided into broad horizontal bands; this time the vertical element holding everything together is the triangular shape of the lifting gear. Unusual elements in this picture are the amount of human activity Sisley has included and the surprisingly strong and bright colours he has used.

∧ Cows on the Banks of the River Seine at Saint-Mammès *c* 1886

Pastel

SISLEY MANAGES here to include two favourite subjects – the river and farming life – in one picture as he sketches a girl keeping an eye on two cows as they graze by the river; in the background, the river life also continues, with two small boats on the water and a large barge over by the far bank. Sisley is working with pastel, a medium of strong colours used unmixed, applied over what appears to be a brown paper; this has enabled him to give some warmth to the cold colours of his picture – notably the light blue of the sky.

▷ The Loing Canal and Church at Moret 1886

Oil on canvas

SISLEY HAS SO COMPOSED this painting that the eye is lead directly to the ancient church of Notre Dame, one of the great churches of the Ile de France (near which, incidently, Sisley would choose to live when his family returned to Moret-sur-Loing in 1889). His backdrop is a summer sky of light cloud and delicate blue. At this time, despite having had his work shown to an American audience in Durand-Ruel's first New York Impressionist exhibition in l885, Sisley was feeling so out of sympathy with other painters of the Impressionist group that he refused to show any of his work in the eighth and last Impressionist Exhibition in Paris in l886. From now on he would devoted himself to working away quietly in the countryside around Moret.

◁ **The Bridge of Moret-sur-Loing** 1887

Oil on canvas

CONTEMPORARY photographs tell us that this is a remarkably faithful account of the buildings, including mills, around the stone bridge at Moret, as they were in Sisley's time, though the point at which he has set up his easel means that the mill (the pink-toned building with shutters immediately to the right of the bridge) obscures a long section of the many-arched bridge. By now, Sisley was totally involved in painting the medieval town of Moret, with its many ancient buildings, watchtowers and town walls, behind which nestled a donjon and the great church of Notre-Dame. Several of the town's buildings would provide Sisley with the subjects for the 'series' paintings he had become interested in early in the 1880s.

▽ **The Bridge at Moret** 1888

Oil on canvas

MORET-SUR-LOING may have been quite an important town in its heyday, having been part of the dowries of two queens of French, but by the time Sisley came to live there it was a sleepy little place whose reminders of former glories made it an attraction for tourists visiting the forest of Fontainebleau. In this painting, Sisley emphasizes the town's present quiet rather than its historic past, adding to the peaceful country air by including two cows and a few geese on the river bank.

▷ **September Morning** 1888

Oil on canvas

HERE IS SISLEY at his most delicately lyrical, giving us his impression of the Ile de France countryside at a particularly lovely time of year, when the almost too green shades of summer are giving way to the gentler hues of early autumn. The painting is very pastoral in atmosphere, carrying on a theme which had run through Sisley's work since he had come to the Loing and started a series of paintings showing Moret viewed from the surrounding hills and countryside. A number of these pictures had made the figure of a young woman a focal point; this picture varies the theme by having a woman in a light-coloured dress and a group of light-coloured buildings as objects of interest. They are not its real focal points, however, for Sisley's unrivalled ability to capture the light of the sky ensures that it is the sky which dominates this picture.

◁ **The Walk** 1890

Oil on canvas

AT THE TIME SISLEY painted this summery scene he had reason to feel much more confident in his future than for many years, for in February he had been invited to take part as an honorary member in that year's exhibition of the Société Nationale des Beaux-Arts, which held its exhibitions at Champ-de-Mars in Paris. Between February and May in 1890 six landscapes by Sisley were shown at the Society's exhibition, to generally very favourable comment. He continued to send pictures to the Society's Champ-de-Mars exhibitions almost every year until his death, thus ending his isolation from the centre of French artistic life.

△ **The Loing Canal** 1892

Oil on canvas.

THE LOING CANAL, a waterway used by working barges, had been cut from the river just north of the centre of Moret-sur-Loing, on a line east of the town. It was the subject of many paintings by Sisley, in all weathers and at all times of year. This particular painting of the canal was one of many offered to the Musée du Luxembourg after Sisley's death in 1899, as part of a gift from Sisley's friends organized by Claude Monet. Sisley returns to a familiar theme – the perspective given a painting by a winding road. Here, the winding road has become the curved lines of the canal and the poplars growing along it, used in such a way that the eye is taken past the house on the far bank of the canal and then back to it, via the curves of the canal.

The Bridge at Moret 1893

Oil on canvas

◁ *Previous pages 72-73*

MORET-SUR-LOING's bridge and the mills built alongside it were painted many times by Sisley, at different times of the year. Although this is a painting of high summer, with a bright blue sky adding a sparkle to the clear waters of the river, it is really a work of the same kind as Sisley's studies of the floods at Port-Marly in early spring, 1876. Here is the same careful balance between water, sky and buildings, their different planes held together by the composition of the picture. Sisley's paintings of the bridge and the buildings surrounding it are now records of things lost. The mills no longer exist and the bridge, badly damaged in World War II, is heavily restored.

▷ The Church at Moret, Evening 1894

Oil on canvas

BETWEEN 1893 and 1895 Sisley painted the Church of Notre Dame at Moret 15 times. This is one of the six studies of the medieval church he did in 1894. Like Monet at Rouen at much the same time, Sisley was intent on recording how different weathers and times of day – that is, different intensities of light – could alter the appearance of the great building and the onlooker's perception of it. Sisley almost always painted the church from the point of view of this picture; it was the angle which best showed the church's size and the sense of monumental timelessness it displayed. Clearly, the church meant a great deal to Sisley. Although he felt himself a Frenchman and had begun to think about taking French nationality, the fact that the great English saint, Thomas à Becket, had connections with this church may have increased Sisley's interest in it. Becket had consecrated the church's choir in 1166, four years before he was murdered in Canterbury Cathedral.

◁ **The Goose Girl** c 1895

Pastel

SISLEY SPENT MOST OF 1895 in Moret, kept there by illness which greatly curbed his activities. It is possible that this pastel was a sketch for an oil painting he had in mind, or it could be that, like Degas, he found pastel an interesting medium to work with after a lifetime of using mostly oil paint. He is again experimenting with the theme of using a winding road or path to give perspective to a picture. This time, however, the picture is not a simple landscape but a study of a person working; the goose girl minding her flock of geese.

△ **Lady's Cove, Wales** 1987

Oil on canvas

SISLEY RETURNED to England for the last time in the summer of 1897, his four-month stay being paid for by a generous industrialist and art patron, François Depeaux. After a brief visit to the south of England, Sisley went to Penarth in Wales, where he found the town 'pretty and the bay, with all the big ships sailing to and from Cardiff . . . superb'. He found a good subject for several paintings in Lady's Cove, Langland Bay. The Cove was dominated by the great Storr Rock, which Sisley painted at different times of day and in different tidal conditions. Here, the rock is surrounded by sea and waves break against it. Whatever his viewpoint, Sisley was always concerned to depict not just the natural objects in front of him but the effect on them of the changing light.

◁ **Morning, Lady's Cove, Langland Bay** 1897

Oil on canvas

IT IS A DELIGHTFULLY sunny summer's day, the sea is luminous, there is a good breeze to send the little sailing ships scudding across the bay, and a small crowd of people have come down to Lady's Cove to enjoy it all, perhaps even going for a swim from the bathing machines drawn up on the shingle. Sisley seems to have enjoyed it all, too, setting it down on his canvas with a lively charm. These paintings in Wales were among the last Sisley did, for after his return to France in November 1897, he managed to complete only another three studies of poplars along the Loing before he became ill with the cancer which was to cause his death in January 1899.

ACKNOWLEDGEMENTS

The Publisher would like to thank the following for their kind permission to reproduce the paintings in this book:

Bridgeman Art Library, London/Cecil Higgins Art Gallery, Bedford 37; /**Christie's, London** 24, 48, 60, 61; /**Fitzwilliam Museum, University of Cambridge** 41; /**Giraudon/Bridgestone Museum of Art, Tokyo** 8-9; /**Giraudon Musée de la Ville, Paris** 46-47; /**Giraudon/Musée des Beaux-Arts, Rouen** 38-39, 77; /**Giraudon/Musée d'Orsay, Paris** 16-17, 19, 20, 32, 40, 44-45, 50; /**Giraudon/Pushkin Museum, Moscow** 58; /**Hermitage, St Petersburg** 42-43; /**Lauros/Giraudon/Musée d'Art et d'Histoire, Palais Massera, Nice** 70; /**Lauros/Giraudon/Musée des Beaux Arts, Agen** 68-69; /**Lauros/Giraudon/Musée d'Orsay, Paris** 72-73; /**Louvre, Paris** 71; /**Musée des Beaux-Arts, Grenoble** 12-13; /**Musée des Beaux-Arts, Le Havre** 66; /**Musée des Beaux Arts, Lille** 30-31; /**Musée d'Orsay, Paris** 14-15, 25, 26-27, 28-29, 35, 54-55; /**National Gallery of Scotland, Edinburgh** 33; /**Private Collection** 10-11, 18, 22-23, 34, 36, 49, 51, 52-53, 56-57, 59, 62, 63, 64-65, 67, 74-75, 76, 78.